Anonymus

A few poems

Anonymus

A few poems

ISBN/EAN: 9783743329263

Manufactured in Europe, USA, Canada, Australia, Japa

Cover: Foto ©ninafisch / pixelio.de

Manufactured and distributed by brebook publishing software
(www.brebook.com)

Anonymus

A few poems

A FEW POEMS

PRINTED FOR THE AUTHOR

SAN FRANCISCO
BACON & COMPANY
1887

TO

G. E. W.

CONTENTS.

WITH A BUNCH OF ROSES.

Lady, accept to mark this day
A poor admirer's poor bouquet :
A bunch of roses all I send,
Yet something fits them for my friend
Better than costly gift of gold ;
For if her praise be truly told,
Her's is the pride, 'mid love of pelf,
To rise above low thoughts of self,
And in a world where self rules all
To hold her self in others' thrall.
Oh, then, behold ! the Queen of flowers—
The Rose that reigns in all earth's bowers—

Heedless of her queenly station,
Sinking self in abnegation,
The humblest subject now would be,
Flower of women, here to thee !

A WINTER SONG.

Red-berried laurel, let me sing
  A little song to thee,
For hearts with happy thoughts upspring
  Beside thy gayety.

England shall praise her holly bough,
  Its glossy green and red ;
But I, who know the holly, vow
  More praises on thy head.

Bright as the flame amid dark pines
  That marks the camp-fire's blaze,—
So bright thy ruddy cluster shines
  Amid dark winter days.

Red as the blood for country's sake
    That stains the soldier's side, —
So red thy cheerful berries take
    Their death for Christmas-tide.

That shapely Redskin of the wood,
    The lithe, smooth-limbed madrone,
Where once, outflushing Youth, it stood,
    Is somewhat pallid grown.

But thou wait'st not for Summer-time
    Among the flowers to please :
As man seeks fame 'mid polar rime
    And scorns soft tropic seas—

So dauntlessly, when many a tree
    Bows down its crownless head,
Thy face is raised for earth to see
    All nature is not dead.

Keep green thy boughs, O cheery tree!
  O cheery tree, keep green!
In darkest days may I, like thee,
  Be ever cheery seen!

.

WITH A DEER'S HEAD.

Take with good will
    Here from a friend,—
Though it but ill
    Suits me to send,—

This souvenir
    Of the wild lake
Where the shy deer
    Stir every brake.

Their's the delight,
    Where nothing bars,
Roaming at night
    Under the stars.

Meeting the day,
 Ghost-like they tread :
Softly as they,
 Move not the dead.

Till on their ears
 Baying of hounds
Falls and with fears
 Spurs them to bounds.

Swifter than fire,
 Heedless of brush,
Hills cannot tire,
 Onward they rush.

Bang!—But the speed
 Laughs in man's face.
Bang!—Shall man's greed
 Mar such a pace?

Safe away !—*Bang!*—
   Death in that shot :
Never more sprang
   Buck from that spot.

What was the gain
   Grace so to mar ?—
(Victory vain !)—
   Horns !   Here they are.

TWO SPRING DAYS.

The West-wind is blowing,
Winter is going;
Kites in the air
Fly everywhere;
The linnet's Spring ditty
Sounds sweet in the city;
Every garden is seen
Now bedecked with new green;
And the hills smiling down
On the toil of the town,
All in sunlight and shade,
Look as soft as the round dimpled cheek of a maid.

Hark !—the fair days are past
And the strengthening blast
Of the West-wind's commotion
Resounds from the ocean !
With clangor terrific,
Across the Pacific,
Driving sea-mists before,
How he leaps to the shore !—
Taking clutch as he lands
Of the granulous sands,
Which he sows without pity
Through fogs on the city,
While the sky every day
Is made dismal with gray,
And the stars every night
Are all blurred out of sight,
And the dust-eddies whirl
Through the streets with a mouth, nose, and eye-filling swirl.

Oh, let skies, as they list,
Change from sunshine to mist !
'Tis no hue of the sky
Paints the world to my eye,
But the warm heart of one
Never dimmed like the sun
On my path casts the shine
Of a sunlight divine.
What to me though a doom
Be in store for Spring's bloom,
Or though never a note
Come from Summer's dry throat ?
In the year that I know,
There is no ebb and flow,
For (all seasons above)
I walk in the warmth and the light of thy love.

LOVE AND SLEEP.

Love heaves the blood like a tide of the ocean
    And sends it in surges to break on the heart :
Sleep spreads a calm o'er the spirit's emotion
    And rocks it to rest only Sleep can impart.

So Sleep hateth Love and will never go nigh to him,
    However Love longingly Sleep would delay :—
All the night long Love may wearily sigh to him,
    Sleep will not hearken, but hastens away.

COWARD DEATH.

Death, how long you were afraid !
   Eager though you were to smite,
   Coward, how you slunk from sight !
All around him though your blade
Cut its swath, it never made
   Move to hurt him, though its might
   Darkened many another's light.
Oh, what tireless joy of living through his limbs
     with rapture played !

But beside him everywhere,—
   By the hearth and in the heather,
   Summer-time and wintry weather,—
Like his shadow, you were there !

Viewless as the empty air,
    Noiseless as a falling feather,
    (Thirty years you two together !)
Watching for a chance to strike him, Coward,
    could you dare.

But you quailed ; for not alone,
    Guardless, on his way he went :
    Two defenders Fate had sent—
Trustier not on man bestown—
Youth and Strength, whose shields were thrown
    Ever toward the least intent
    Barbed with pain or detriment.
And you quailed at their bright prowess and recoiled
    with baffled moan.

O the sight beyond compare—
    Youth and Strength and he together,

Marching through the Highland heather,
In the Hebridean air !
Manhood never shone more fair :
   In the sunny Summer weather,
   Not a heart but (as a feather)
Fluttered to behold him blithe and fearless
      everywhere.

Till, at last, Love joined the band,
   Love that Fate would not assuage :—
   Youth grew thoughtful, then, as Age ;
And from Strength's enfeebled hand
Fell the shield.   Behold him stand
   Stripped and helpless to engage
   Even with a coward's rage !—
Then, O Death, your base invasion cut in two
      life's slender strand !

ON A PIECE OF MUSIC COMPOSED FOR A FRIEND'S WEDDING.

O bridegroom, Music takes her lyre
  And sings her sweetest air,
That all the joy in all our hearts
  May find an echo there.

For Music, mistress of men's souls,
  Has been your mistress too;
And as your joy was honoring her,
  So she would honor you.

TO THE BRIDE.

Had a stranger demanded,—" What have you to show
Of women whose fairness shall not fall below
The fame that belongs to your fruit, flowers, and gold ? "
Then proudly by me had that stranger been told :
   " You should see Isabelle ! "

Had he said,—" Yes, for beauty. But how about brains ?
You gold-diggers give yourselves infinite pains
To fill up your pockets ; but filling the head—
Is there any true culture ? "—Again I had said :
   " Wait and see Isabelle ! "

Had he doubted of manners, I'd pointed to one
The peer of all courtesy under the sun,

Whose speech never otherwise lets her be seen
Than cordial, yet dignified, truly a queen.
        " And her name ? " " Isabelle ! "

And if he had scoffed,—" These are well in their way :
Wit, beauty, and manners—they make their display.
But before they a charm unto life can impart,
You must show me besides them a true woman's heart :"
        My reply,—" Isabelle ! "

Yes, thus had I answered and thus truly thought,
Till the stranger to shame for his doubting was brought ;
But a stranger, too canny to parley or doubt,
Came along and his own eyes spied Isabelle out,
        And he won Isabelle ;

And she leaves us, she leaves—ah, the land of her birth,
For a home at the uttermost parts of the earth,—
A land every day that's as bright as a flower,

For one with the darkness of mists for its dower :
      We have lost Isabelle !

There are warm hearts in Scotland, God knows
      how they 've bled :
For Prince Charles, for Queen Mary what
      heart's blood was shed !
May an equal devotion be thine to the end—
Is the prayer of one always and truly thy friend !
      Fare thee well, Isabelle !

GENIUS DEAD.

" O grave, where is thy victory ? "

Out of darkness into day,
A little while with men to stay,
Loving friends were his alway:
    Now he lies—ah, there !
Like a meteor sped from sight,
Like a lost love's past delight,
Like his laughter yester-night—
    He is gone—ah, where?

But his work remains behind,
Deathless offspring of his mind,
Humanizing all mankind
    By the light it gives.

Oh, then, mourners, dry your tears !
Conquered are the coming years ;
See how paltry Death appears :
    He is dead, yet lives !

ON THE EVE OF A VOYAGE.

O thou who for two years hast filled my mind
   More than the thought of all the world beside,
   Making the days no longer to divide
In measurements which science has divined—

Since it is sunrise when I see thee first,
   And sunset when at last thou say'st Good Night,
   Or when thy windows cease to flash the light
Which for thy presence partly stills my thirst:

Dear heart of hearts, one kiss and then farewell !
   I give my body to the rolling sea;
But will not still a thousand omens tell,
   My soul meets nightly in this wood with thee?

THE ABSENT SAILOR.

EXCERPTS FROM A NARRATIVE POEM.

I.

Bedimmed with long, vain scanning of the sea,
Her eyes take lustre as her musings roam
To Cornwall, his high, sea-lashed, thunderous home:—

O Cornwall, rocky Cornwall !
    Thy men are stout and brave,
They take life's buffets like thy cliffs
    That front the western wave.

O Cornwall, sunny Cornwall !
    Where Spring comes early and fair,—
There are no lovelier maids than thine
    In England anywhere.

O Cornwall, royal Cornwall !
  Mother of maids and men,—
There Tristram died for Iseult's sake :
  Ah, sorely love smote then !

O Cornwall, happy Cornwall !
  Let my love *live* for me,
And let me live to see his child
  Sit smiling on my knee !

II.

Then on the sands she poured this wailing forth :
To whom ? if not, lost lord of her heart, to thee,—
Strong son of Cornwall, somewhere on the sea :

  Where art thou now, my Cornish heart ?
    No sail is on the sky,
  The sea spreads trackless out of sight,
    The wind goes speechless by.

I've watched a hundred ships come in,
   A hundred ships go out ;
But watching only breaks my heart,
   It cannot.quell my doubt.

Perhaps the wave that's at my feet
   Has felt thy vessel's keel :
Oh, give me, God, the power to guess
   One word it could reveal !

Perhaps yon star that lights the pole
   Shines where thou, too, canst see :
Oh, might our glances meet therein
   And tell me, love, of thee !

Where art thou now, my Cornish heart ?
   Till this be answered true,
For me there is not peace nor sleep
   Nor anything but rue.

IN THE GRAVE.

They bid me join them at the dance,
  They bid me with them riding go,
They chide me for my mirthless glance
  And say, " He was not always so."
But oh, what now can give me mirth?
My love is dead,—she lies in earth.

They never knew her heart was mine,
  Without a sigh they called her dead;
But oh, I would that Death's design
  Had laid me in the same cold bed.
Away, away, and have your mirth:
My love is dead,—she lies in earth.

That dear, true heart beneath the sod—
   Oh, might I, like the rest, believe
She sleeps but till we meet in God :
   Then lightly could I cease to grieve !
But nothing now can bring back mirth :
My love is dead,—she lies in earth.

WAGNER: A MEMORIAL ODE.

I.

Dead, say they? Deathless one,
Live as the living sun,
Life-giver, world-waker,
Soul-smiting cloud-breaker,
Quickening with fiery might
Hearts faint with worldly blight,
Warming cold seeds of thought
Which else had sprung to nought,
Waking to second birth
Beings long laid in earth,
First, in all human ken,
Master of souls of men,—
So long as lives the sun,
Livest thou, deathless one!

2.

Ah, but thou speak'st no more, thy last word's said :
This power alone has dull Death on thy head,—
Voiceless to be, in voice so like a God ;
Wordless, whose words leapt as with lightning shod.
To see thee mute—ah, Fate, what is the gain
That lips like his should motionless remain ?
Is it for love you let Death smite him so—
Love that would fain his peerless voice forego,
If him unwearied it might thereby save
From yelping critics harrying to the grave?
Or is it envy of that generous heart
Who royally fulfilled his royal part,
And once more hallowed the cheap name of king
By lifting above strife, serene to sing,
Him, of all sons his native country bore,
Greatest of men since Goethe spoke no more?

Or was it fear, O Fate, that let Death smite?
Fear lest your sway should suffer in earth's sight,
If men too long unhindered might rejoice,
Mindless of you, to follow his sole voice?—
Sweet as the peace of two hearts love makes one,
Joyous as sunshine, glad as Easter sun,
Strong as sea surges, weak as clinging vines,
Harsh as the tramp of wind through mountain pines,
Tender as blossoms, soft as maiden lip,
Fierce as foam leaping on a foundering ship,
Radiant as smiles upon an infant's face,
Keen as the bent bow springing back to place,
Stern as the law of life, mild as the dove,
Pale as dawn starlight, red as flaming love.
Ah, me! that voice is mute, those cold lips sealed :
How much is left unsaid will never be revealed.

3.

Ah, but Death *has* not won,
Shall not win, deathless one,
Thee to his shadow-land.
And though his pallid hand
Freeze thy lips' fiery word,
Still shall thy voice be heard
Loud on the lips of those
Who at thy will arose,
Scatheless of Death's design,
Quickened by breath of thine.
They hold the soul of thee
Now for eternity,—
Life-giver, world-waker,
Soul-smiting cloud-breaker,
So long as lives the sun,
Livest thou, deathless one !

BALLAD OF THE NORTH-WIND.

Hark! on the lake the North-wind hunts
   And drives his wintry pack,—
A thousand foaming hounds before,
   The North-wind at their back.

His brother Frost rides by his side,
   Armèd with arrows frore:
Was ever baying heard till now
   Voiced like the ocean's roar?

Whence come they?   From high Shasta's snow,
   Far in the unseen North,
Bent on their winter's ravening,
   The twain fared keenly forth.

With a bound they leapt from Shasta's side,
  And wild the pace they rode,
And many a mountain barrier
  Their galloping bestrode.

And through the land as on they passed,
  A furrow, like a frown,
Marked where the thick-set mountain pines
  Were trod and trampled down.

Until at last Elk Mountain rose.
  Then with a fierce delight,
Quicker than powder springs to flame
  They reached its topmost height.

There in a whirlwind they stood still.
  Poised in the cloudless air,
Like eagles, moveless, they beheld
  The goal that lured them there.

Konockti's lake rimmed round with hills
   Gleamed in the wintry sun :
As stars fall, with one headlong swoop
   The water's marge was won.

Lo ! at the touch the North-wind's hounds, —
   That sleep beneath the lake,
Loosened their tongues in such a note
   As the last trump shall make.

Hark ! though the sun long set should bid
   The huntsman's speed grow slack—
Hark ! on the lake the North-wind hunts
   And drives his wintry pack.

The stiff trees bend as the hunt goes by,
   The trees blanched bare like bones ;
Thicker than once last year with leaves
   Their boughs are filled with moans.

The wild fowl fly before the blast
    Like fluttering Autumn leaves;
With beak and claw and steadying wings,
    The owl to the pine-top cleaves.

Clangor of hard swords clashed in fight,
    Clangor of human wail,
Wrung from a city that's wrapped in fire,
    Before this clangor pale.

Ah, but the dawn !—Its earliest gleam
    Beheld the still lake hushed.
Back to his jagged Shasta clefts
    The wild North-wind had rushed.

But lo ! still here, his brother Frost,
    A-weary with the chase,
On high Konockti's summit sits
    And rests him for a space.

Gladder than lovers' eyes he grew
    On that aërial stand,
As his wide-circling glance surveyed
    Glory of lake and land.

Joy at his heart he felt exhale
    Like perfume out of flowers,
Till thought was dimmed of that far home
    Where gathering thunder lowers.

But then uprose the swift red sun
    And aimed his fieriest ray :
As deer start at the fateful note
    When hounds strike scent and bay—

Frost vanished ; and on Shasta's side,
    Safe from the withering sun,
The rent rocks marked the bound he made :
    The winter's chase was done.

www.ingramcontent.com/pod-product-compliance
Lightning Source LLC
Chambersburg PA
CBHW032136080426
42733CB00008B/1101